HOME AWAY FROM HOME

THE VANCOUVER TONARI GUMI COOKBOOK

TG BOOKS

Printed and bound in Canada by Friesens, Altona, Manitoba. Typeset in Futura, Times, News Gothic Standard, Kozuka Gothic Standard and Impact.

First Edition, June 2007
Second Printing, November 2010
Third Printing, June 2011

Library and Archives Canada Cataloguing in Publication. Includes index.

ISBN: 978-0-9783378-0-3

Jell-O® is a registered trademark of Kraft Foods Holdings, Inc. Rice Krispies® is a registered trademark of the Kellogg Company.

Japanese Community Volunteers Association
511 East Broadway
Vancouver, British Columbia, Canada
V5T 1X4
t. 604.687.2172   f. 604.687.2168
www.jcva.bc.ca   info@jcva.bc.ca

English Editorial Team: Kikko Tasaka, Joji Kumagai, Richard Yasushi Ii
Japanese Editorial Team: Sayuri Sugawara, Junko Takashima

Seniors Program Coordinator: Sayuri Sugawara
Cookbook Project Coordinators: Richard Yasushi Ii, Sayuri Sugawara
Test Kitchen Coordinators: Kikko Tasaka, Sayuri Sugawara
Translation: Mari Kato, Keiko Funahashi
Photography: Richard Yasushi Ii, Hideaki Anzai
Design and Layout: Richard Yasushi Ii
Japanese Calligraphy: Kazuko Ikegawa
Home Away From Home Website: Chika Okamura

Cookbook Test-Kitchen Workshop Team:
Sayuri Sugawara, Kikko Tasaka, Tam Tanaka, Kazuki Takashima, Atsuko Shuto, Mariko Suzuki, Etsuko Takata, Toshiko Koriyama, Tomoko Li, Harry Kishi, Shizuko Mikurube, Satomi Matsuoka, Yuka Matsuno, Junko Takashima, Yoshiko Shimizu, Naomi Su, Yukie Tateyama, Tomiko Noda, Asako Nomura, Mitsuko Inomata, Alice Maeda, Seiko Karakama, Hiroyo Kitano, Motoko Reed, Kazu Matsukura, Yoshie Omura, Shoko Nakagawa, Mitsuko Kawashima, Kimiko Hayashi, Kimiko Higashi, Ying Kan, Kumiko Mori, Kanako Kokubun, Miyuki Maekawa, Emiko Matsui, Natsuko Fujii, Yuriko Uyeda

If you would like more information regarding Tonari Gumi's programs and services, please contact us.

ACKNOWLEDGEMENTS

The Japanese Community Volunteers Association (Tonari Gumi) would like to acknowledge the assistance and generosity of the following organizations and local businesses that helped make this project possible:

Human Resources & Skills Development Canada's New Horizons For Seniors Program
Angel Seafoods Ltd.
The Canadian Fishing Company (Canfisco)
Amano Foods Ltd.
Fugeta Family Farm (Kalden, British Columbia)

SPECIAL THANKS TO

In Memoriam: Roger Ryunosuke Watanaka (1928 - 2011)

We would also like to thank the following individuals for their patient support, advice and time in helping us to achieve our goal:

Tam Tanaka, Atsuko Shuto, Kazuki Takashima, Junko Takashima, Keisuke Sato, Egidio Spinelli, Kayoko Nishioka, Mari Kato, Harry Kishi, Pearl Williams, David Iwaasa, Miko Hoffman and the Powell Street Festival Society, Vincent, Jessica and Matisse Law, Estella Lum and everyone else who generously contributed in ways large and small.

Tonari Gumi would like to extend a special thanks to Richard Yasushi Ii and Sayuri Sugawara who made the corrections and additions necessary to update this third printing and to the many individuals throughout the Lower Mainland and throughout Canada who helped to ensure the first & second printings were fully sold out and gave us courage to go to another printing. Appreciation for on-going support is extended to the current staff of Tonari Gumi (David Iwaasa, Sayuri Sugawara, Junko Takashima and Shihori Scott-Moncrieff) and the Tonari Gumi Board of Directors led by Derek Iwanaka, Chairperson.

創

CONTENTS

THE RECIPES

FORWARD
まえがき

It is with sincere gratitude to the generosity of our sponsors and contributors that we, at the Japanese Community Volunteers Association (Tonari Gumi) here in Vancouver, have been able to come together for the creation of this cookbook.

Tonari Gumi has always been a place where many people from all walks of life have gathered. It was only fitting that we had this wonderful opportunity for seniors and volunteers to gather together and enjoy testing recipes. We are very grateful to everyone who shared their favorite recipes, some in memory of friends who have passed on. Many recipes are from the local Japanese-Canadian community that have been either lost or forgotten, so this was a great opportunity for the seniors to revive and pass them on to a new generation of cooks. We have tried our best to use recipes that are simple and nutritious.

If you have any questions or you need help please do not hesitate to contact us. We do hope this book will be enjoyed by all!

Lurana Kikko Tasaka
Seniors Advisory Committee

"Community recipes that have either been lost or forgotten..."

"Tsukuru" by Kazuko Ikegawa

ABOUT TONARI GUMI
隣組について

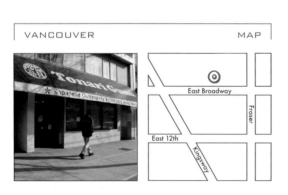

VANCOUVER   MAP

East Broadway

Fraser

East 12th

Kingsway

Over 35 years ago, Tonari Gumi, or the Japanese Community Volunteers Association was established by Jun Hamada to help struggling Japanese-Canadians living in the area within Vancouver once known as "Japan Town". Nurtured through the years by its dedicated staff and volunteers, Tonari Gumi came to offer a variety of cultural, educational and senior based programs, congregate lunches, outings and services such as help in dealing with various governmental organizations, interpretation and translation. With its warm and welcoming atmosphere, it truly became a "home away from home" for many Japanese-Canadians.

However, Tonari Gumi is constantly adapting to meet the different needs of a changing community. Drawing from the same basic principles of grassroots volunteerism which motivated the founders of Tonari Gumi, new programs such as meals-on-wheels, the Telephone Buddy Program and others have been initiated to meet the needs of a rapidly changing population. Many of the programs within Tonari Gumi benefit from the on-going support of the Vancouver Coastal Health Authority, the Vancouver City Community Services Grants, the New Horizons for Seniors Program of Human Resources and Skills Development Canada, the Consulate-General of Japan, the United Way and many individual and corporate sponsors. Indeed, the

first printing of this cookbook was developed thanks to the assistance provided under Human Resources and Skills Development Canada's New Horizons for Seniors Program. Under that program, Tonari Gumi seniors had the opportunity to share their recipes and experiences with younger volunteers, passing on their heritage to the next generation. In purchasing this new printing of our "Home Away From Home" cookbook, you are helping Tonari Gumi to continue enriching the lives of our seniors and the many others who come to Tonari Gumi seeking help and assistance. Tonari Gumi is committed to following in the footsteps of its predecessors and ensuring that the bridge between the past and the present is still strong.

The Staff and Volunteers of Tonari Gumi

1	4
2	
3	5
	6

1] Seniors Christmas party
2] Staff at work
3] Broadway entrance
4] Common area
5] Powell Street Festival
6] Lunch program

11

CHAPTER ONE

SALADS 創

HAKUSAI SALAD

白菜サラダ

HOME AWAY FROM HOME

SERVES 6-8

2 pkgs.	ramen noodles, crumbled
1 tbsp.	butter
1 cup	walnuts, chopped
1 tsp.	curry powder
1 pkg.	ramen soup base
1 medium	hakusai, finely sliced

Dressing:

½ cup	vegetable oil
½ cup	sugar
¼ cup	vinegar
1 tbsp.	soy sauce
to taste	salt & pepper

1 Over medium heat, fry ramen noodles with butter and add walnuts, curry powder and soup base. Allow to slightly cool.

2 Combine ingredients for the dressing and season with salt and pepper to taste.

3 Just before serving, combine hakusai, noodle mixture and dressing as the salad is best when the noodles are crispy. Mix well.

[See page 27 for tips on how to choose hakusai.]

SERVES 8

1 can = 540 ml

1 can	green beans
1 can	yellow beans
1 can	kidney beans
1 can	lima beans
1 cup	celery, chopped
½ cup	red onions, sliced
½ cup	green peppers, sliced

Mustard dressing:

½ cup	vegetable oil
½ cup	vinegar
½ cup	sugar
1 tsp.	dry mustard
1 tsp.	oregano
to taste	salt, pepper & garlic salt

1 Rinse and drain beans.

2 Mix beans, celery, red onion and green pepper.

3 Combine dressing ingredients and season with salt, pepper and garlic salt. Mix with beans and vegetables. Best served at room temperature.

BEAN SALAD

ビーンサラダ

SALAD WITH NATTO DRESSING
納豆ドレッシングサラダ

SERVES 4-6

½ cup	chives
1 bunch	spinach
¼ cup	dried wakame
2 cups	daikon, shredded or cut into thin, long strips
3 cups	bean sprouts

Natto dressing:

1 pkg.	natto
1	red chili pepper, seeded & finely chopped
1 clove	garlic, grated
¼ cup	vinegar
2 tbsp.	soy sauce
2 tbsp.	sesame oil
1 tbsp.	miso

1 Blanch chives and drain.

2 Flash boil spinach in salt water. Drain and squeeze excess water out. Cut both spinach and chives into 3-5 cm pieces.

3 Soak wakame in cold water and cut into bite-sized pieces.

4 Rub salt into daikon (shio-momi) and squeeze excess water out.

5 Combine natto dressing ingredients and mix well.

6 Mix chives, spinach, wakame, daikon and bean sprouts and serve with natto dressing.

1 pkg.	soba (360 g.)
4	long sticks of imitation crab meat
2	eggs
2	Japanese cucumbers, cut into thin, long strips
2 tbsp.	nori, shredded
1 tbsp.	white sesame seeds

Wasabi dressing:

3 tbsp.	mayonnaise salad dressing
1 tbsp.	wasabi paste
2 tbsp.	vinegar or lemon juice
to taste	salt & pepper

1 Boil soba until al dente. Rinse very well and drain.

2 Peel crab sticks into long strips and cut in half.

3 Beat eggs and fry into thin, crepe-like pieces. Cut into thin strips.

4 Combine wasabi dressing ingredients and mix until wasabi is dissolved.

5 Mix soba and dressing. Garnish with crab, cucumber and egg.

6 Sprinkle shredded nori and sesame seeds on top just before serving.

SOBA SALAD

蕎麦サラダ

DAIKON SALAD WITH MISO DRESSING

大根の味噌ドレッシングサラダ

SERVES 6

1 head	lettuce, sliced
1 small	daikon, shredded
1 bunch	red radish, sliced
½ cup	green onions, finely chopped

Miso dressing:

½ cup	vinegar
⅓ cup	vegetable oil
⅓ cup	miso
½ cup	mayonnaise salad dressing
2 tbsp.	sugar
2 tbsp.	mirin
2 tbsp.	sesame oil

1 Combine lettuce, daikon, red radish and green onions.

2 Mix miso dressing ingredients until miso is dissolved. Add to vegetables just before serving.

Shred or slice:

1 cup	green cabbage
1 cup	red cabbage
1 cup	red pepper
½ cup	carrots
1 cup	Japanese cucumber

Chop:

4 stalks	green onions
1 cup	broccoli
1 cup	bean sprouts
2 pkgs.	ramen noodles, crumbled
½ cup	sliced almonds
¼ cup	white sesame seeds
1 pkg.	ramen soup base
1 tbsp.	butter

Dressing:

2 tbsp.	sugar
⅓ cup	vegetable oil
1 tsp.	salt
½ tsp.	pepper
½ cup	vinegar
1 pkg.	ramen soup base
2 tsp.	soy sauce

1 Put vegetables, including bean sprouts, in a large bowl and chill in refrigerator for about an hour.

2 Fry ramen noodles, almonds, sesame seeds and soup base with butter over medium heat.

3 Combine and mix ingredients for the dressing.

4 Just before serving, mix all ingredients with the dressing. The ramen noodles should be crispy when salad is served.

CRUNCHY RAMEN SALAD

カリカリパリパリサラダ

CARROT RAISIN SALAD

キャロットレーズンサラダ

HOME AWAY FROM HOME

SERVES 4

4 cups	carrots, grated
1 cup	raisins
4 tbsp.	mayonnaise

1 Mix carrots with raisins and then add mayonnaise. That's it!

隣組

Choosing Hakusai

Hakusai (Japanese cabbage) can be used for salads, tsukemono, hot pots, miso soup and stir-frys. When choosing hakusai, look for relatively heavy ones with white bottoms and closed leaves. Avoid hakusai with black dots on the lower white parts of the leaves as this indicates the hakusai is not fresh. When storing the vegetable, wrap with newspaper, stand upright and leave in a dark place. Hakusai will keep for 2 to 3 weeks. Once it is cut, wrap with plastic wrap and store in the refrigerator.

4 cups	broccoli florets
1	small can of water chestnuts, sliced
½ cup	raisins or grapes
½ cup	green onions, chopped
½ cup	roasted sliced almonds

Dressing:

1 cup	mayonnaise
¼ cup	sugar
2 tbsp.	vinegar

1 Mix broccoli, water chestnuts, raisins and green onions and refrigerate overnight.

2 Combine ingredients for the dressing. Mix well.

3 Mix dressing with broccoli mixture. Top with almonds just before serving.

BROCCOLI SALAD

ブロッコリーサラダ

NANA'S LAYERED SALAD

レイヤーサラダ

SERVES 8-10

1 head	lettuce, chopped
3 cups	frozen peas, slightly boiled before layering
1 bunch	spinach, chopped
2	small cans of water chestnuts, sliced
6 stalks	green onions, chopped
6	eggs, boiled & sliced
2 tsp.	bacon bits (optional)

Dressing:

1½ cups	mayonnaise
1 tsp.	curry powder
2 tbsp.	sugar

Layer each item separately in a glass bowl as follows:

1 lettuce, half
2 boiled peas
3 spinach
4 water chestnuts
5 lettuce, half
6 green onions
7 eggs
8 salad dressing
9 bacon bits

Leave salad overnight in the refrigerator before serving.

About a 9 inch wide and 6 inch deep glass salad bowl is recommended for this salad as each layer should be visible.

1 pkg.	lemon Jell-O® powder
1 cup	boiled water
1 block	tofu (350 g.)
½ cup	Japanese cucumber, thinly sliced
1 bunch	red radish, sliced
2 stalks	green onions, chopped
½ tsp.	salt
½ tsp.	pepper
¼ cup	mayonnaise
2 tbsp.	lemon juice

1 Dissolve lemon Jell-O® powder in boiled water. Allow to cool but do not chill.

2 Remove excess water out of tofu by applying light pressure with a plate for 30 minutes. Puree tofu in a food processor.

3 Rub extra salt into cucumber (shio-momi). Squeeze excess water out. Repeat procedure for red radish.

4 Mix all ingredients and add to Jell-O® mixture. Pour into a salad mold and chill in refrigerator until Jell-O® sets.

CHAPTER TWO

JAPANESE PICKLES
TSUKEMONO

HAWAIIAN-ZUKE

ハワイアン漬け

HOME AWAY FROM HOME

SERVING SIZES VARY

5-6	medium daikon
2¾ cups	sugar
¼ cup	salt
½ cup	vinegar
½ tsp.	tumeric powder

1 Cut each daikon lengthwise into quarters. Slice into quarter circles.

2 Combine sugar, salt and vinegar in a large bowl. Dilute tumeric powder in a little water and mix in.

3 Add daikon to the vinegar mixture and leave covered for a few days to allow flavour to blend.

Tsukemono

A variety of condiments such as salt, miso or soy sauce can be used to make tsukemono, not just vinegar. The pickles are easy to make, retain nutrients and can be served with rice. Pickling also takes the harshness and bitterness from vegetables. Other than members of the potato family, most vegetables can be pickled. When using vinegar to make tsukemono, use komezu if possible (see page 41 for more information on types of Japanese vinegars).

1 large	hakusai
3 tbsp.	salt
1 medium	daikon, shredded
1 medium	carrot, shredded
6 stalks	green onions, chopped
1	small piece of konbu (about 3 cm by 3 cm)
2 cups	water

Chili pepper mixture:

1 tbsp.	honey
2 tbsp.	ami
1 tbsp.	chili pepper powder
2 cloves	garlic, grated
1 tbsp.	salt

1 In a large bowl, cut hakusai lengthwise into quarters and sprinkle with salt. Place a plate on top and apply even pressure such as with water bottles for about a day or so.

2 Remove hakusai, rinse slightly and squeeze out excess water. Place hakusai along with other vegetables in a large, flat-bottomed, rectangular container and set aside.

3 In a pot, soak konbu in water and leave for about 30 minutes. Cook over medium heat until water is reduced to about 1½ cups. Remove konbu.

4 When cooled, add chili pepper mixture ingredients and mix well. Pour into container over vegetables and mix.

5 Leave for about 3 days in refrigerator. Cut into bite-sized pieces and serve.

KIMCHI
キムチ

CUCUMBER TSUKEMONO

きゅうりの漬物

HOME AWAY FROM HOME
SERVING SIZES VARY

2	Japanese cucumbers, sliced
1 tsp.	salt
2 tbsp.	vinegar
2 tbsp.	mirin
4 tbsp.	soy sauce
3 cm piece	ginger, peeled & grated

1 Sprinkle cucumbers with salt. Set aside for 1 hour. Remove cucumbers and squeeze out excess water. Check taste. If cucumbers are very salty, wash to remove excess salt.

2 Mix vinegar, mirin, soy sauce and grated ginger.

3 Place cucumber slices into soy sauce mixture and leave for about 15 minutes before serving.

Japanese Vinegars

There are three main types of Japanese vinegars: kokumotsusu (grain vinegar), komezu (rice vinegar) and sushizu (sushi vinegar). Kokumotsusu is made from wheat, corn or other types of grains and can be drizzled over fish or meat when cooking to soften the meat up. Komezu helps keep vegetables and prevents discolouring so it's ideal for pickling. It is also used to make sushi vinegar from scratch. Sushizu is vinegar with the ingredients needed to make sushi vinegar, such as sugar and dashi, already mixed in so all that is needed is to add to rice. Sushizu can also be used as is or with a little soy sauce as a salad dressing.

41

½ **medium**	hakusai, sliced
½ **medium**	cabbage, sliced
2	Japanese cucumbers, sliced
3 **medium**	carrots, shredded
1 **large**	daikon, shredded
1	broccoli head, chopped into florets
2 **cups**	water
½ **cup**	sugar
½ **cup**	vinegar
¼ **cup**	salt
2 **cloves**	garlic, grated
2 **tbsp.**	ginger, grated

1 Combine vegetables in a large bowl.

2 Mix water, sugar, vinegar and salt in a pot. Bring to a boil.

3 Cool off and pour onto vegetables. Add garlic and ginger. Mix well.

4 Keep cool in a container for a few days.

5 Squeeze out liquid by hand and serve.

VEGETABLE TSUKEMONO

野菜の漬物

BIYAZUKE
ビール漬け

SERVING SIZES VARY

2 cups	miso
1 bottle	beer
⅔ cup	vinegar
¼ cup	salt
⅔ cup	sugar

Suggested Vegetables:

Daikon, carrots, eggplants, Japanese cucumbers, etc.

1 Combine miso, beer, vinegar, salt and sugar in a large, flat-bottomed, rectangular container. Mix until miso is dissolved.

2 Cut daikon into quarters lengthwise. Cut carrots and eggplants in half lengthwise. Cucumbers can be left whole.

3 Soak vegetables in miso mixture for at least a day.

4 Remove vegetables from mixture and wash. Cut into bite-sized pieces before serving.

Note: Inexpensive miso can be used. The mixture can be used more than once. However, after a few uses it could become watery so scoop out the water from the top and add the seasoning ingredients as needed.

CHAPTER THREE
SIDE DISHES 創

KIMPIRA GOBO

きんぴらごぼう

HOME AWAY FROM HOME

SERVES 4

Gobo is also known as Burdock Root

2 cups	gobo, shredded - see step 1
2 tbsp.	sesame oil
1 cup	carrots, shredded
1	chili pepper, seeded and chopped
1 tbsp.	white sesame seeds

Seasoning:

3 tbsp.	soy sauce
1 tbsp.	sake
1½ tbsp.	sugar
1 tbsp.	mirin
¼ cup	water
1 tsp.	dashi-no-moto

1 Soak gobo in water immediately after shredding. Drain just before frying.

2 For seasoning, combine ingredients and mix well.

3 Heat sesame oil and fry gobo over medium-high heat for about 5 minutes. Add carrots and cook for another 3 minutes.

4 Add chili pepper and seasoning mixture. Simmer over medium-low heat until sauce is gone.

5 Sprinkle white sesame seeds on top and serve.

1 slice	white bread, crusts removed
¼ cup	water
¼ tsp.	dashi-no-moto
3 tbsp.	sugar
½ tsp.	mirin
¼ tsp.	salt
4	large eggs

1 Soak bread in water and add dashi-no-moto, sugar, mirin and salt. Mix with beater or blender until mixture is well blended and bread crumbs are not visible.

2 Add one egg at a time to above mixture and blend well.

3 Lightly oil a square 9 by 9 inch pan on all sides. Pour egg mixture to approximately a 1 cm thick level and cook on low heat with lid on for about 8 minutes or until cooked. Flip over and cook for about 10 seconds. Alternatively, the egg mixture can be baked in an oven at 180°C for about 15 minutes.

4 Place cooked egg mixture on a bamboo sushi mat with the darker side up. Roll tightly.

5 Hold roll with rubber bands and leave for a few hours.

6 Remove rubber bands and bamboo sushi mat and cut roll into 1 cm thick pieces and serve.

Note: Instead of bread, a ½ cup of surimi (ling cod fish paste) can also be used.

DATEMAKI

伊達巻き

OKARA
おから

SERVES 4-6

2 medium	carrots
6 medium	dried shiitake mushrooms
¼ block	konyaku
2 pieces	abura-age
1 tbsp.	vegetable oil
1½ cups	okara
1 tbsp.	sesame oil
3 stalks	green onions, chopped

Seasonings:

¼ cup	sugar
5 tbsp.	soy sauce
1 tsp.	mirin
1 cup	water
1 tsp.	dashi-no-moto
1 tbsp.	vegetable oil

Okara is a by-product during the production of soy milk. Some stores give okara away or charge a very cheap price for it.

1 Soak shiitake in water until soft. Drain.

2 Finely chop carrots, mushrooms, konyaku and abura-age. Cook over medium heat with vegetable oil for 4 minutes.

3 Add seasonings and stir for 1 minute.

4 Add okara. Mix well and cook until okara is crumbly.

5 Simmer on low heat to allow sauce to evaporate, and then turn off heat.

6 Add sesame oil and green onions, lightly mix and serve.

2 lbs.	green beans
1 tbsp.	vegetable oil
1 lb.	peeled prawns (optional)

Sauce:

2 cups	onion, chopped
2 cloves	garlic, grated
2 tbsp.	black bean sauce
2 tbsp.	brown sugar
2 tbsp.	miso
2 tbsp.	oyster sauce
¼ cup	soy sauce
1 tbsp.	sesame oil

1 Put sauce ingredients into a food processor and mix until creamy.

2 Cut beans in half and fry in vegetable oil over high heat for about 5 minutes.

3 If using prawns, add and cook for an additional 1 or 2 minutes.

4 Reduce heat to medium. Add sauce and cook again for another 2 or 3 minutes. Serve hot.

隣組

Serving Tip

To make a meal more authentic, use several small dishes, one for each item rather than one large plate per person.

SAMBAL BEANS

インゲンのサンバルソース炒め

MISO SAUCE EGGPLANTS

なす田楽

SERVES 4

2 large Japanese eggplants
6 tbsp. vegetable oil
as needed poppy seeds (optional)

Miso Sauce:

¼ cup miso
3 tbsp. sugar
⅓ cup mirin

1 Mix miso sauce ingredients in a pot and cook over medium heat, stirring slowly with a wooden spatula until smooth. Do not let sauce burn.

2 Trim stem from eggplants. Cut eggplants lengthwise into halves. Cut shallow notches along the cut surface.

3 Heat oil in a pan over medium heat. Place eggplants cut surface down and cook with lid on. Turn over a few times until tender. Drain off excess oil.

4 Spread miso sauce on top while eggplant is still hot. Garnish with poppy seeds if desired and serve.

Edamame are also known as soy beans.

1 lb.	edamame, removed from pods & frozen
½ cup	soy sauce
1 tsp.	dashi-no-moto
3 cm piece	ginger, peeled & grated
¼ cup	mirin

1 Thaw frozen edamame in colander with lukewarm water. Drain well.

2 Mix together soy sauce, dashi-no-moto, ginger and mirin.

3 Add edamame and set aside for at least 1 hour to allow soy sauce mixture to be absorbed, and then serve.

Water & Tofu

Removing excess water from tofu can increase flavour absorption and make tofu easier to handle. One simple way is to place tofu on a plate, microwave for 2 - 3 minutes and pat the excess water off with a paper towel.

EDAMAME

枝豆

TOFU SHIRA-AE

豆腐白和え

SERVES 4-6

1 bunch	spinach
3 medium	dried shiitake mushrooms
1 block	konyaku, cut into 1 cm wide strips
3 medium	carrots, grated

Tofu mixture:

1 block	tofu (350 g.)
¼ cup	white sesame seeds, ground
1 tbsp.	sesame oil
3 tbsp.	miso
2 tbsp.	sugar
to taste	salt

1 Flash boil spinach. Drain and squeeze out excess water. Cut into 3 cm lengths.

2 Soak shiitake until soft. Drain and finely slice.

3 Place konyaku strips in a colander. Pour boiling water over top.

4 Blanch carrots for about 2 minutes. Drain.

5 For tofu mixture, first remove excess water out of tofu by applying light pressure with a plate for 30 minutes. Mash tofu until smooth. Add sesame seeds, sesame oil, miso and sugar. Sprinkle in salt to taste. Mix well.

6 Combine and mix spinach, shiitake, konyaku, carrots and tofu mixture and serve.

CHAPTER FOUR

MEAT DISHES 創

CHICKEN TESSEN
のし鶏鉄扇

SERVES 4

1 lb.	boned chicken
1 medium	onion
2	eggs
3 tbsp.	sugar
3 tbsp.	soy sauce
2 tbsp.	cornstarch
as needed	sesame seeds

Sauce mixture:

3 tbsp.	mirin
2 tbsp.	soy sauce
1 tbsp.	sugar

1 Preheat oven to 180°C.

2 Combine sauce ingredients and stir over medium heat until sugar dissolves and sauce slightly thickens. Remove from heat and set aside.

3 Put chicken, onion, eggs, sugar, soy sauce and cornstarch into a food processor and blend until a paste.

4 Lay parchment paper on a baking sheet and spread chicken paste, 1 cm thick, on top.

5 Bake in oven for about 15 minutes.

6 Brush sauce onto the baked chicken paste and bake for another 2 - 3 minutes.

7 Repeat 2 or 3 times until surface is slightly browned. Remove from oven and sprinkle on sesame seeds.

8 Cut into fan shapes, skewer with tooth-picks and serve.

MEAT DISHES

1 lb.	boned chicken
4 tbsp.	soy sauce
2 tbsp.	mirin
4 cloves	garlic, grated
2 tsp.	ginger, grated
as needed	cornstarch
as needed	vegetable oil, for deep-frying

1 Cut chicken into bite-sized pieces.

2 Add soy sauce and mirin to garlic and ginger and mix well.

3 Marinate chicken in sauce for about an hour.

4 Toss chicken in cornstarch until chicken is coated. Deep-fry in 180°C vegetable oil until well done.

CHICKEN KARA-AGE

鶏の唐揚げ

STUFFED TERIYAKI CHICKEN
まんぷくテリヤキチキン

HOME AWAY FROM HOME

SERVES 4

3	chicken breasts
to taste	salt & pepper
as needed	flour
3 cups	cabbage, shredded
2	boiled eggs, chopped
1 tbsp.	vegetable oil

Teriyaki sauce:

2 tbsp.	soy sauce
1 tbsp.	sugar
1 tbsp.	sake
1 tbsp.	mirin

1 Combine teriyaki sauce ingredients and mix until well blended. Set aside.

2 Cut chicken breasts apart while ensuring halves are still joined in the middle. Pound with tenderizer to make thin.

3 Sprinkle salt, pepper and flour on one side of the chicken.

4 Turn chicken over and place cabbage and eggs on top. Roll chicken and toss in flour until all sides are covered.

5 Heat oil in pan at medium heat. Cook seam of the roll first to prevent roll from coming apart. When well-cooked, cook the rest of the roll until it is crispy.

6 Add teriyaki sauce. Roll chicken back and forth in pan to absorb sauce. After 1-2 minutes, the sauce will thicken.

7 Remove roll from pan and cut into bite-sized pieces. Spoon leftover sauce onto rolls and serve.

1 lb.	boned chicken, sliced into large pieces
1 tbsp.	oregano
1 tsp.	salt
1 tsp.	pepper
1 tsp.	garlic, grated
1 tbsp.	vegetable oil
1 cup	onions, diced
½ cup	sour cream
1 can	cream of mushroom soup (284 ml)
½ cup	milk

1 Preheat oven to 180°C.

2 Rub chicken with oregano, salt, pepper and garlic. Leave for about 15 minutes, and then brown over vegetable oil.

3 Combine onions, sour cream, soup and milk in a baking pan. Place chicken in mixture.

4 Bake in oven for ½ - 1 hour until chicken is cooked. Serve hot.

CHICKEN WITH CREAM SAUCE

鶏肉のクリームソース

DRUMSTICKS & DAIKON

鶏肉と大根の煮物

SERVES 4

10-12	chicken drumsticks
1 medium	daikon
12 pieces	konbu (each about 3 cm by 1 cm)
4 cm piece	ginger, peeled & shredded
1 cup	brown sugar
1 cup	soy sauce
½ cup	sake

1 Gently poke holes into drumsticks with a fork to allow meat to absorb sauce. Pour hot water over chicken.

2 Cut daikon in half lengthwise. Cut halves into 1 cm thick, semi-circular pieces.

3 Place chicken, daikon, konbu and ginger in a pot. Add enough water to soak ingredients.

4 Boil then reduce heat to low and skim off top. Add brown sugar, soy sauce and sake. Cover directly with aluminum foil and simmer for about 1½ hours. (otoshibuta)

5 Turn off heat and leave for 15 minutes to allow flavours to blend before serving.

[See page 77 for otoshibuta]

SERVES 12

Yakibuta is Japanese-style roasted pork.

4 lbs. (approx.) pork tenderloin
1 tbsp. vegetable oil

Sauce:

1 cup soy sauce
4 pieces garlic, grated
2 medium onions, diced
2 bay leaves
3 cloves, crushed
2 tsp. ginger, grated
3 tbsp. sugar
⅔ cup wine
1 cup water

1 Preheat oven to 180°C.

2 Cut pork lengthwise so that each piece is about 5-7 cm thick. Fry with vegetable oil over medium-high heat until all sides are browned.

3 Combine sauce ingredients together and mix well.

4 Place fried tenderloin and sauce in a baking dish and simmer in oven for about 1 hour, turning meat every 15-20 minutes so that meat absorbs sauce.

5 Slice, spoon sauce over meat and serve.

Halve the recipe for a smaller serving size. The left-overs can be frozen and used in fried rice or ramen.

YAKIBUTA
焼豚

SESAME MISO PORK

揚げ豚のごま味噌ソース

SERVES 4

¾ lb.	thinly sliced pork
½ tsp.	soy sauce
1 tbsp.	sake
as needed	cornstarch, for dipping pork slices
as needed	vegetable oil, for deep-frying
as needed	white sesame seeds

Sesame miso sauce:

½ tsp.	soy sauce
2 tbsp.	sake
2 tbsp.	sesame paste
1 tbsp.	miso
2 tsp.	sugar
1 tsp.	sesame oil
2 tbsp.	mirin
1 clove	garlic, grated
3 cm piece	ginger, peeled & grated
3 stalks	green onions (optional), chopped
1 tsp.	tobanjan

1 Cut pork slices into approximately 7 - 10 cm long pieces and marinate in soy sauce and sake for 30 minutes.

2 Mix all ingredients for sesame miso sauce and mix well.

3 Lightly coat pork in cornstarch and deep fry in 180°C vegetable oil until cooked.

4 Toss pork slices in sesame miso sauce until paste evenly covers the meat. Sprinkle with sesame seeds and serve.

Otoshibuta

Otoshibuta is a technique where foil or a lid is placed directly on top of ingredients that are being braised. There are two main benefits of doing so as opposed to simply placing a lid on the pot. One is the sauce will trickle down on the ingredients leading to better flavour assimilation. The second benefit is fish, potatoes, daikon and other delicate ingredients will be less disturbed so once cooking is finished, they will come out intact.

½ lb.	lean ground pork
2 cloves	garlic, chopped
2 tbsp.	vegetable oil
1½ lbs.	prawns, peeled & cut in half, lengthwise
½ cup	water
2 tbsp.	black bean sauce
2 tbsp.	soy sauce
1 tsp.	sugar
1 tbsp.	cornstarch
3 stalks	green onions, chopped
2-3	eggs, beaten

1 Sauté ground pork with garlic in vegetable oil at high heat until well-done.

2 Add prawns and cook for an additional 2 minutes.

3 Add water. Cover and simmer for approximately 5 minutes at low heat.

4 Add black bean sauce, soy sauce and sugar.

5 Dilute cornstarch in a little water and stir into above.

6 Add green onions.

7 Slowly pour in eggs and slowly stir for about a minute or until eggs appear fluffy. Serve hot.

GROUND PORK/PRAWNS IN BLACK BEAN SAUCE

挽肉とエビの黒豆ソース炒め

STUFFED ZUCCHINI WITH GROUND PORK
ズッキーニのはさみ揚げ

SERVES 3-4

2 medium	zucchini
to taste	salt & pepper
as needed	flour
as needed	vegetable oil, for deep-frying

Filling:

½ lb.	ground pork
4 tbsp.	breadcrumbs
1	egg, beaten
½ tsp.	dry basil
½ tsp.	dry oregano
½ tsp.	salt
pinch	pepper

Coating:

as needed	flour
1	egg, beaten
1 cup	breadcrumbs

1 Slice zucchini into 5-6 mm thin circles. Sprinkle with salt and pepper.

2 Fry ground pork without oil in a non-stick fry pan at medium-high heat. When pork is cooked, allow it to cool.

3 Add breadcrumbs, egg, basil, oregano, salt and pepper to ground pork. Mix well.

4 Place two slices of zucchini on counter top and sprinkle flour on sides facing up. Spread pork mixture on one zucchini piece covering evenly and place the other zucchini piece on pork mixture, flour-side down so that pork mixture is sandwiched in between zucchini pieces. Repeat with other zucchini slices.

5 Coat zucchini with flour and dip in egg. Then coat with breadcrumbs and fry in 170°C vegetable oil until surface becomes crispy.

6 Cut in half and serve.

4 medium	sweet potatoes
1 cup	cooked ham, chopped into small pieces
1 cup	carrots, shredded
½ cup	green onions, chopped
to taste	salt & pepper
as needed	vegetable oil, for deep-frying

Coating:

as needed	flour
1	egg, beaten
1-2 cups	breadcrumbs

1 Bake sweet potatoes in oven until done. Peel and mash.

2 Mix together potatoes, ham, carrots and green onions.

3 Season with salt and pepper.

4 Ready egg, flour and breadcrumbs for coating sweet potato mixture by having each in a separate bowl.

5 Take a tablespoonful of sweet potato mixture and form a ball. Coat in flour and dip in egg. Next, coat with breadcrumbs. Repeat as necessary.

6 Take one korokke ball and deep fry in 180°C vegetable oil until browned. Ensure oil is hot enough to prevent korokke from crumbling apart.

HAM/SWEET POTATO KOROKKE

ハムとさつま芋のコロッケ

1 bunch	spinach
12 pieces	thinly sliced beef
as needed	flour
to taste	salt & pepper
½ cup	cheddar cheese, grated

Serve as an hors d'oeuvre or as a main dish. Asparagus can be used instead of spinach.

1 Preheat oven to 180°C.

2 Flash boil spinach, drain and squeeze out excess water.

3 Line up 4 slices of beef side by side on a cutting board. The slices will form the roll so ensure there is a little overlap. Sprinkle on flour, salt and pepper.

4 Place spinach across a short side of the beef. Roll slices of beef into a large roll. Cut into approximately 6 pieces.

5 Lay beef rolls in an oven pan and place cheese on top. Season with salt and pepper.

6 Place the pan onto the middle rack of the oven and cook for approximately 15 minutes or until beef is cooked.

BEEF & SPINACH ROLLS

牛肉のほうれん草巻き

PARTY-TIME SPECIALS 創

BARBECUE TIME
バーベキュータイム

SERVES 6 / RECIPE
Barbecue Time with Shish Kebabs

ASIAN D'LITE WITH PEANUT SAUCE

1 lb. meat (chicken, beef, or pork), cut into bite-sized pieces

as needed vegetables (mushrooms, onions, peppers or any other vegetables of your choice), cut into bite-sized pieces

Sauce:

½ cup soy sauce
½ cup creamy peanut butter
2 tbsp. brown sugar
2 tsp. curry powder
3 cloves garlic, crushed

1 Combine the sauce ingredients and mix well.

2 Marinate meat in sauce for a few hours.

3 Alternately thread meat and vegetables onto skewers.

4 Char-grill or barbecue skewers for 4-5 minutes or until meat is cooked. Baste with leftover sauce when cooked.

∽

FISH WITH MISO MARINATE

1 lb. fish (preferably salmon), cut into bite-sized pieces

as needed vegetables (green onions, green peppers, etc.), cut into bite-sized pieces

Sauce:

½ cup miso
⅓ cup brown sugar
½ cup beer

1 Mix all ingredients for sauce until miso is dissolved.

2 Marinate fish in sauce for one day.

3 Alternately thread fish and vegetables onto skewers.

4 Char-grill or barbecue skewers for 4-5 minutes or until fish is cooked. Baste with leftover sauce when cooked.

HAWAIIAN FISH D'LITE

1 lb.   fish (cod, halibut or any other white fish), cut into bite-sized pieces

as needed   pineapple chunks & banana

Sauce:

½ cup   mayonnaise
1 tbsp.   lemon juice
1 tsp.   curry powder
½ tsp.   tumeric powder (optional)

1 Combine sauce ingredients and mix well. Do not marinate with this sauce.

2 Alternately thread skewers with fish and fruit.

3 Char-grill or barbecue skewers for 4-5 minutes or until fish is cooked. Baste several layers while cooking.

SEAFOOD D'LITE

1 lb.   scallops
1 lb.   prawns

as needed   vegetables (green onions, onions, cherry tomatoes, or any other vegetables that cook very easily), cut into bite-sized pieces

Sauce:

⅓ cup   soy sauce
2 tbsp.   sugar
1 tsp.   ginger, grated

1 Mix all ingredients for sauce.

2 Marinate scallops and prawns for at least 1 hour.

3 Thread scallops, prawns and vegetables alternately onto skewers.

4 Char-grill or barbecue skewers for 4-5 minutes or until seafood is cooked. Baste with leftover sauce when cooked.

BARBECUE TIME
バーベキュータイム

BARBECUE TIME
バーベキュータイム

SERVES 6 / RECIPE
Barbecue Time with Shish Kebabs

MEATBALL SHISH KEBABS

Meatballs:

1 lb.	ground beef
1	egg
½ cup	green onions, chopped
½ cup	breadcrumbs
as needed	vegetables (potatoes, zucchini, onions, or any other vegetables of your choice), cut into bite-sized pieces

Sauce:

½ cup	tomato ketchup
⅓ cup	brown sugar
1 tbsp.	lemon juice

1 Preheat oven to 180°C.

2 Combine meatball ingredients and mix well. Make 15-20 meatballs, and pre-cook in oven for about 30 minutes.

3 Mix sauce ingredients together and set aside.

4 Alternately thread meatballs and vegetables onto skewers.

5 Char-grill or barbecue skewers for 2-3 minutes or until vegetables are cooked. Baste with sauce.

Required ingredients are:

beef thinly sliced, can be bought frozen

seafood prawns, scallops, squid, etc. or seafood of your choice

vegetables onions, bean sprouts, asparagus, beans, eggplants, peppers or vegetables of your choice

tofu cut into small blocks

Teppanyaki is a wonderful recipe for a nice dinner party at home. It's a guaranteed hit if the guests are having Japanese food for the first time! An electric grill or gas burner is required as all the ingredients are cooked at the table by the guests.

Discretion will be needed as far as quantity is concerned. On two large platters, arrange beef, seafood and vegetables and place a platter on each side of the grill. Have vegetable oil on hand for grilling. As the beef, seafood and vegetables cook, dip into a sauce before eating. Please refer to page 97 for a list of teppanyaki sauce recipes.

[Contined on page 97]

BEEF & SEAFOOD TEPPANYAKI

鉄板焼き

BEEF & SEAFOOD TEPPANYAKI

鉄板焼き

SERVING SIZES VARY

TEPPANYAKI SAUCE RECIPES

Sauce 1:

2 tbsp.	white sesame seeds, ground
3 tbsp.	sugar
1 tbsp.	miso
½ cup	soy sauce
1 tbsp.	vinegar
1 tsp.	chili oil
1 tsp.	garlic, grated
1 tsp.	ginger, grated
1 stalk	green onion, finely chopped

Mix all ingredients well.

Sauce 2:

1 tbsp.	ginger, grated
2 cups	onions, chopped
¾ cup	soy sauce
¼ cup	vinegar
½ cup	sugar

Put in blender and mix well.

Sauce 3:

1 cup	daikon, grated
4 tbsp.	soy sauce
2 tbsp.	lemon juice

Mix all ingredients well.

Sauce 4:

½ cup	soy sauce
¼ cup	vinegar
3 tbsp.	sugar
2 tsp.	powdered mustard

Mix all ingredients well.

Crepe mixture (for 8 crepes):

1½ cups	water
½	egg
2 tsp.	mirin
1 cup	flour

Ingredients for 1 portion:

1 cup	cabbage, finely shredded
¼ cup	green onions, chopped
½ cup	bean sprouts
¼ cup	tenkasu
⅓ cup	seafood (e.g. shrimp, squid, or scallops, etc.)
2-3 slices	pork, thinly sliced
½ pkg.	soft yakisoba noodle
½ pkg.	yakisoba sauce
1	egg

1 To make crepe batter, combine 1 cup water, egg and mirin and mix well.

2 Add flour and mix until the batter is smooth.

3 Add remaining ½ cup of water and stir well. Set aside for 1 hour in refrigerator.

4 Oil a frying pan or grill. Pour about ¼ cup of batter to make a crepe.

5 On top of crepe, add cabbage, green onions, bean sprouts, tenkasu, seafood and lastly meat.

6 Drizzle 2 tbsp. of batter on top of meat.

7 Cook until bottom is slightly browned. Flip with two spatulas so filling faces down.

8 Cook until cabbage is translucent and in the meantime, to the side of the pan or grill, or on another frying pan, cook yakisoba with its packaged sauce.

9 Once cabbage is cooked, place entire crepe over yakisoba and lightly apply pressure to flatten crepe a little.

10 On the side, or another frying pan, fry egg. Break yolk and spread a little. Next, lift crepe and yakisoba and place on egg.

11 Flip crepe over so that the egg is on top.

12 Cut into 4 pieces. Okonomiyaki is traditionally served with tonkatsu or okonomiyaki sauce. Okonomiyaki can also be topped with mayonnaise, kezuribushi and aonori before serving.

HIROSHIMA OKONOMIYAKI

広島風お好み焼き

CHAPTER SIX
FISH & SEAFOOD DISHES

SALMON MISONNAISE
サーモン味噌ネーズ

SERVES 4

4	salmon fillets
as needed	vegetable oil, for basting
to taste	salt & pepper
2 tbsp.	green onions or chives, chopped

Misonnaise sauce:

6 tbsp.	mayonnaise
2 tbsp.	miso

1 Preheat oven to broil.

2 Combine misonnaise sauce ingredients together and set aside.

3 Baste a little oil on salmon fillets and season with salt and pepper.

4 Broil skin side first until cooked. Turn over and broil the other side.

5 Spread misonnaise sauce on top of each fillet and broil again for only a minute or so, until surface browns slightly.

6 Garnish with green onions or chives and serve.

Note: For a large party or as a potluck dish, use a whole salmon, preferably sockeye. Cut the salmon lengthwise, leaving it whole and de-bone the entire fish. Double the ingredients for the misonnaise sauce. Make sure that the fish is oiled slightly so that it does not stick to the pan when turning it over.

FISH & SEAFOOD DISHES

HOME AWAY FROM HOME
SERVES 8

3-4 cups	fish paste (chum or pink salmon) – see step 1
3	eggs
4 tbsp.	sugar
1 cup	cornstarch
1 cup	water
1 tbsp.	salt
1 cup	gobo, finely chopped
1 cup	carrots, finely chopped
1 cup	green onions, finely chopped
2 tsp.	sesame seeds
as needed	vegetable oil, for deep-frying

1 Remove skin and bones from salmon. Cut into small pieces and put in food processor. Blend well to make paste.

2 Put salmon paste in a bowl and mix while adding eggs.

3 Add sugar and mix again.

4 Dilute cornstarch in water and add to mixture. Mix until firm.

5 Add salt and mix.

6 Add gobo, carrots, green onions and sesame seeds and mix until well combined.

7 Shape fish paste as desired, and deep-fry in 170°C vegetable oil.

Note: Adding a tablespoon each of miso and sesame oil in step 5 will enhance the taste.

SATSUMA-AGE
さつま揚げ

SMOKED SALMON COULIBIAC

スモークサーモンの包み焼き

SERVES 8

1 bunch	spinach
¼ cup	fresh dill, finely chopped
1 lb.	sliced smoked salmon
4	eggs, hard-boiled & sliced
1 cup	sour cream
to taste	pepper

Pastry:

12 sheets	phyllo pastry
¼ cup	melted butter

Onion filling:

2 tbsp.	butter
2 large	onions, diced
2 cloves	garlic, grated
1 cup	breadcrumbs
½ cup	parmesan cheese
1 tsp.	Dijon mustard

1 Preheat oven to 190°C.

2 Flash boil spinach. Drain, squeeze out excess water and chop. Set aside.

3 For filling, melt butter, add onions and garlic and sauté for 3-4 minutes. Add breadcrumbs, parmesan cheese and Dijon mustard. Mix well and set aside.

4 On a cookie sheet, lay one sheet of phyllo and brush with melted butter. Place next phyllo sheet on top and brush with melted butter. Repeat until all 12 phyllo sheets are used.

5 Leave approximately a 5 cm border from the edges of the pastry and spoon onion filling in an 8 cm wide, horizontal strip over phyllo. Proceed to layer ingredients in the following order: dill, sliced smoked salmon, egg slices, spinach and sour cream. Add pepper to taste.

6 Roll pastry to make a long cylinder. Tuck in ends and brush roll with melted butter. Poke holes along top of pastry with a fork.

7 Bake for about 30 minutes or until browned. Cut into pieces and serve.

Note: Phyllo pastry can be bought frozen at groceries stores or at any Greek food stores. Regular pie pastry can also be used instead of phyllo pastry.

2 large	crabs
2 tbsp.	vegetable oil

Sauce:

2	eggs
1 tbsp.	garlic, grated
1 tsp.	ginger, grated
2 tbsp.	black bean sauce
1 tsp.	sugar
to taste	yellow paste from crab shell

1 Cut up crab. Save the yellow paste found in the large shell. This will be used for the sauce. Make sure live crabs are purchased the same day crab is to be served.

2 Combine sauce ingredients, mix well and set aside.

3 Fry crab in a wok over high heat with vegetable oil for 5 minutes.

4 Keeping heat at high, cover wok with a lid and steam crab for approximately 5-10 minutes, stirring occasionally. Do not let it overcook.

5 Lower heat to medium. Mix sauce with crab, steam again for a few minutes and serve.

CRABS IN BLACK BEAN SAUCE

カニの黒豆ソース炒め

SALMON & OKARA KOROKKE
サーモンとおからのコロッケ

SERVES 4-6

Filling:

1 can	sockeye salmon, drained
3 cups	okara
1½ cups	breadcrumbs
1 cup	carrots, shredded
½ cup	green onions, chopped
2 tsp.	salt
1 tsp.	pepper
1	egg
2 tbsp.	sesame oil

Coating:

1	egg
3 tbsp.	milk or cream
as needed	breadcrumbs
as needed	vegetable oil, for deep-frying

1 Mix all filling ingredients together. Add more breadcrumbs if needed until mixture is firm enough to be able to shape.

2 For coating, mix egg with milk and prepare breadcrumbs separately in a bowl.

3 Take a tablespoonful of filling, form a ball, dip into egg and milk mixture and coat with breadcrumbs.

4 Deep-fry in 180°C vegetable oil until coating browns.

Making Dashi

Two of the more popular types of dashi are kombu dashi and katsuo dashi. Konbu dashi is a vegetarian option for recipes that require dashi.

Konbu dashi

4 cups water, 30 g. konbu

If there is a whitish powder on the konbu, don't wash it off as the dashi will taste better if it is included. Add water and konbu in a pot over medium heat. As the water almost begins to boil, skim the top and remove konbu. The dashi is now ready.

Another method is to simply leave konbu in water for 10 hours.

Katsuo dashi

4 cups water, 40g. kezuribushi

Boil water and as boiling point is reached, add kezuribushi and turn off heat. Skim top and wait until flakes settle to the bottom. Filter flakes from the soup stock.

2 tbsp.	lemon juice
2	fillet of whole salmon cut lengthwise, de-boned with skin on
to taste	black pepper
1 cup	coarse salt
1 cup	sugar
1 cup	brown sugar
1 cup	dill, roughly chopped
½ cup	parsley, roughly chopped

1 Rub lemon juice on fillets and sprinkle with pepper.

2 Mix salt, sugar and brown sugar together and press on to the meat side of fillets.

3 Mix dill and parsley and press on top of salt and sugar mixture.

4 Flip meat side of fillets together like a sandwich with skins toward outside.

5 Put in a large plastic bag or cover with plastic wrap to cover fillets.

6 Place in a large pan and press with a light weight such as a plate for 12 hours.

7 Flip over and again, apply weight for 12 hours. Repeat process for each side.

8 Cure for about 2 days. Thinly slice. Serve only the meat of fillets and not the skin.

Note: For best results, sockeye salmon should be used. This dish is the Scandinavian version of smoked salmon or sashimi. Always a great hit at potluck parties.

SALMON GRAV-LOX

サーモングラブロックス

SURIMI ROLL
すり身ロール

SERVES 8

Ingredients listed below are the quantities required to make 4 rolls.

1 bunch	spinach
4 sheets	nori
4 cups	surimi (ling cod paste)
6 tbsp.	sakura denbu

Atsuyaki-tamago:

4	eggs
½ tsp.	salt
1 tbsp.	sugar

1 Flash boil spinach. Drain and squeeze out excess water.

2 To make atsuyaki-tamago, mix eggs with salt and sugar. In a lightly oiled fry pan, add ⅓ of egg mixture and cook over medium heat. Once egg begins to dry a little, roll towards one end of fry pan. With roll still in fry pan, pour another third of egg mixture and cook until mixture dries a little. Roll first mixture toward the other end of the fry pan, picking up and rolling the second mixture together in the process. Pour last third and again, once mixture dries a little, roll large roll to the other end of fry pan, picking up and rolling the third mixture together in the process. Place on cutting board and cut in strips.

3 To make one surimi roll, place one sheet of nori on a bamboo sushi mat and spread surimi over nori sheet except for a 3 cm strip across the top. Next, place atsuyaki-tamago, sakura denbu and spinach across nori about ⅓ the way up. Roll carefully.

4 Keep bamboo mat wrapped around roll and hold with about three elastic bands. Repeat to make three more rolls.

5 With elastics on, steam rolls for about 15 minutes.

6 Remove, and separate rolls from bamboo mats immediately. Leave rolls to cool. Cut and serve.

1 cup	broccoli florets
½ small	kabocha, sliced
3 medium	carrots , sliced
1 lb.	prawns, peeled
1 tbsp.	vegetable oil

Sauce:

6 tbsp.	mayonnaise
2 tsp.	mustard
2 cloves	garlic, grated
to taste	salt & pepper

1 Boil broccoli, kabocha and carrots for a few minutes.

2 Blanch prawns and drain.

3 Combine mayonnaise, mustard and garlic and season with salt and pepper. Mix well.

4 Fry vegetables in vegetable oil over high heat.

5 Reduce heat to medium, add prawns and sauce and stir for 2 minutes. Serve hot.

PRAWN & BROCCOLI STIR-FRY

エビとブロッコリーの炒めもの

CHAPTER SEVEN

RICE & PASTA DISHES

CHIRASHI SUSHI
ちらし寿司

HOME AWAY FROM HOME

SERVES 10

* The rice measurement calls for a Japanese cup which is equivalent to 180ml or ¾ of a regular cup.

5 cups*	Japanese rice
10 medium	dried shiitake mushrooms
5 medium	carrots, grated
2 sticks	chikuwa fish cakes, chopped
1 cup	water
3 tbsp.	soy sauce
½ tsp.	dashi-no-moto
3 tbsp.	sugar
1	renkon, thinly sliced
8	eggs
1 cup	green peas
3 tbsp.	sakura denbu
5	long sticks of imitation crab meat, shredded
to taste	nori, cut into strips

Sweet vinegar mixture:

½ cup	vinegar
1½ tbsp.	sugar
½ tsp.	salt

Vinegar mixture:

½ cup	vingear
½ cup	sugar
½ tsp.	salt

1 Wash rice, soak in water for ½ hour and then cook.

2 Soak shiitake mushrooms until soft, and then chop.

3 Combine shiitake mushrooms, carrots and chikuwa in water. Add soy sauce, dashi-no-moto and sugar and cook for about 10 minutes. Set aside.

4 Combine sweet vinegar mixture ingredients.

5 Boil renkon in hot water for about 5 minutes. Drain and then soak in sweet vinegar mixture for flavoring.

6 Beat eggs, fry into paper-thin crepes and cut into strips.

7 Boil green peas slightly.

8 Combine vinegar mixture ingredients and mix into cooked rice. Let it cool.

9 Squeeze out liquid from shiitake mixture and mix cooked ingredients into rice. Add sakura denbu and mix. Drain renkon and mix in.

10 Just before serving, garnish with egg, imitation crab and nori.

SERVES 6

* The rice measurement calls for a Japanese cup which is equivalent to 180ml or ¾ of a regular cup.

4 cups*	Japanese rice
4 cups*	water
1 cup	konyaku
1 tsp.	dashi-no-moto
1 tbsp.	sake
1 tbsp.	soy sauce
1 tsp.	salt
6 medium	dried shiitake mushrooms
1 cup	carrots, chopped
1 cup	green peas
1 can	sockeye salmon, drained

1 In rice cooker, wash rice and soak in water for ½ hour. Set aside.

2 Chop konyaku into small pieces. Place in a colander and pour hot water over top.

3 Add dashi-no-moto, sake, soy sauce and salt to rice.

4 Soak shiitake mushrooms until soft and then chop.

5 Add konyaku, shiitake mushrooms, carrots and peas to the rice. Mix together.

6 Break salmon into little chunks and put on top of the rice.

7 Cook rice. When cooked, mix and let it steam for about 10 minutes before serving.

SALMON MAZE GOHAN

鮭のまぜご飯

SEKIHAN

赤飯

HOME AWAY FROM HOME

SERVES 3–4

½ cup	azuki
3 cups	water
2 cups	mochi-gome
to taste	salt
as needed	black sesame seeds

1 Boil azuki in 3 cups water until soft but not too soft. Drain but save water. Ladle water and pour back into water container several times from a small height. Allowing the water to come in contact with the air will improve the colour of the sekihan.

2 Wash mochi-gome and drain. Put into a casserole dish.

3 Take 1⅓ cups of azuki water and pour into casserole dish. If there is not enough azuki water, top up with water to 1⅓ cups. Soak mochi-gome for about an hour.

4 Add azuki to rice, cover and microwave for about 10 minutes.

5 Mix, cover and microwave for another 6 minutes.

6 Mix again, cover with wet cloth and let it stand.

7 Sprinkle with salt and black sesame seeds and serve.

SERVES 6

* The rice measurement calls for a Japanese cup which is equivalent to 180ml or ¾ of a regular cup.

3 cups*	Japanese rice
1 cup	abura-age
1 cup	water
3 tbsp.	soy sauce
1½ tbsp.	sugar
1-2 cups	matsutake mushrooms, chopped
1½ tsp.	salt
2 tbsp.	sake
1 tsp.	dashi-no-moto

1 Wash rice and soak in water for ½ hour. Then, in a colander, drain water and set aside.

2 Pour hot water over abura-age to drain off fat, and then finely chop.

3 Mix water, soy sauce, sugar, abura-age and mushrooms in a pan and cook at low heat for about 10 minutes.

4 Squeeze and save the liquid out of the above mixture. Add enough water to the liquid to make 3 Japanese cups or 540 ml.

5 Put drained rice in a rice cooker and add the above 3 Japanese cups of liquid. Add salt, sake and dashi-no-moto. Mix and then cook.

6 When rice is done, place abura-age and mushroom mixture onto the cooked rice, cover and let it simmer for about 10-15 minutes. Mix and serve.

Note: Matsutake mushrooms are seasonal so freeze them when available. Fresh shiitake mushrooms, other mushrooms, bamboo shoots, etc. can be substituted.

MATSUTAKE GOHAN

松茸ご飯

UNAGI SUSHI

うなぎ寿司

SERVES 4-5

* The rice measurement calls for a Japanese cup which is equivalent to 180ml or ¾ of a regular cup.

3 cups*	Japanese rice
1 pkg.	barbecued unagi
1 bunch	spinach

Vinegar mixture:

⅓ cup	vinegar
2 tbsp.	sugar
1 tsp.	salt
½ tsp.	dashi-no-moto

Crepe:

6	eggs
½ tsp.	salt
1 tsp.	sugar
2 tbsp.	cornstarch, slightly diluted

1 Wash rice, soak in water for ½ hour and cook.

2 Combine and mix vinegar mixture ingredients.

3 Cut unagi into long strips.

4 Flash boil spinach, drain and squeeze out excess water. Leave in long strips.

5 Mix eggs, add salt, sugar and cornstarch.

6 In a well-greased fry pan, add egg mixture to make a thin crepe. Rotate pan to make sure egg is well spread and of even thickness. Flip over and leave just for a minute. Make 4-5 crepes.

7 Put cooked rice in a bowl and mix with vinegar mixture. Let it cool.

8 Place 1 egg crepe on a bamboo sushi mat. Spread rice on egg crepe and place unagi and spinach across rice about ⅓ the way up. Roll firmly.

9 Cut into small pieces and serve.

SERVES 4-6

* The rice measurement calls for a Japanese cup which is equivalent to 180ml or ¾ of a regular cup.

3 cups*	Japanese rice
8	prawns
8 medium	dried shiitake mushrooms
1 cup	water
½ tsp.	dashi-no-moto
½ tbsp.	sugar
1 tbsp.	soy sauce
1 tbsp.	sake
2	eggs
2	egg yolks
½ tbsp.	mirin
pinch	salt
8 slices	smoked salmon (5 cm by 5 cm)

Vinegar mixture:

⅓ cup	vinegar
1 tsp.	salt
2 tbsp.	sugar

1 Wash rice, soak in water for ½ hour and cook. Combine ingredients for vinegar mixture and mix into cooked rice. Make 32 balls of rice and set aside. Eight pieces each of 4 types of sushi will be made: prawn, shiitake, egg and salmon.

2 Boil prawns in hot water with salt for a few minutes. Cool, peel and slice into two lengthwise.

3 Soak shiitake mushrooms until soft. Cook with water, dashi-no-moto, sugar, soy sauce and sake.

4 Combine eggs and egg yolks and add mirin and salt. Scramble slightly.

5 For smoked salmon, remove excess oil with paper towels.

6 Prepare a sheet of plastic wrap. Take one split prawn and place halves side to side but with head pointing in opposite directions. Ensure pink side is face down on the wrap. Next, place a ball of rice on top the prawn. Wrap tightly and shape into a ball.

7 The same can be done with smoked salmon and shiitake mushroom. With the scrambled eggs, gently pat egg on top of rice.

TEMARI SUSHI

手まり寿司

CURRY RICE
カレーライス

HOME AWAY FROM HOME

SERVES 8

1 tbsp.	vegetable oil
1 lb.	pork or beef
1 tsp.	salt
4 cloves	garlic, grated
2 cups	onions, diced
4 cups	water
3 medium	carrots, chopped
2	green peppers, chopped
2	red peppers, chopped
1	turnip **or**
4	medium-sized potatoes, chopped
1 cup	peas or beans
1 box	medium hot curry roux (8 servings)

1 Heat vegetable oil in a pot. Cook pork or beef with salt over medium-high heat until well-browned.

2 Add garlic and onions and cook well.

3 Add water and rest of vegetables.

4 Cook until vegetables are done and add curry roux cubes. If it is too thick, add water. If too watery, add diluted cornstarch. Serve with rice.

2	avocado
1 clove	garlic, minced
2-3 tbsp.	vegetable oil
¼ cup	butter
1 cup	chicken (optional), diced
1	red pepper, chopped
1	yellow pepper, chopped
4	button mushrooms, sliced
¼ cup	flour
2 cups	chicken stock, warm
4 tbsp.	parmesan cheese
½ cup	whipping cream
to taste	salt & pepper

1 Blend avocado, garlic and vegetable oil in a blender. Set aside.

2 Warm butter over medium heat and sauté chicken, red and yellow peppers and mushrooms. Reduce heat to low and add flour to sautéed vegetables. Combine well.

3 Gradually pour warm chicken stock into vegetables and stir well. Increase heat to medium.

4 Add avocado mixture into the pan and stir until combined.

5 Add the parmesan cheese and whipping cream and stir well.

6 Season with salt and pepper and continue stirring for a few minutes.

7 Serve on pasta.

AVOCADO CREAM SAUCE

アボカドクリームソース

CLAM SAUCE
クラムソース

HOME AWAY FROM HOME

SERVES 4

1 can	clams (284 ml)
2 tbsp.	butter
2 clove	garlic, grated
2 tbsp.	parsley, chopped
1 can	cream of mushroom soup (284 ml)
¼ cup	milk
2 tbsp.	parmesan cheese, grated

1 Drain clams, but save ¾ cup of the clam juice.

2 Melt butter in saucepan over medium heat and cook clams, garlic and parsley for 2-3 minutes.

3 Stir in cream of mushroom soup, milk, clam juice and cheese.

4 Reduce heat to low and cook for about 5 minutes.

5 Serve over rice or pasta.

Japanese Rice

Japanese rice is short-grain. The quality of the rice is based on its taste, colour, lustre and stickiness. Four well-known, authentic rice varieties are koshihikari, akitakomachi, hitomebore and sasanishi-ki. These varieties can be found in Japanese food stores. North American brands of Japanese rice are either short-grain or medium-grain. Readily available brands are Kokuho Rose, Nishiki and Tamaki. Another type of rice which is more glutinous than Japanese rice, is called mochigome and is used to make mochi and sekihan.

6 tbsp.	black sesame seeds, ground
4 tbsp.	soy sauce
6 tbsp.	parmesan cheese, grated
to taste	salt & pepper
1 pkg.	spaghetti (360 g.)
1 tbsp.	white sesame seeds

1 Put black sesame seeds in a medium bowl and add soy sauce. Mix well. Add cheese and season with salt and pepper.

2 Boil spaghetti until al dente but do not discard water. Take ½ cup of the boiled water and add to the sesame mixture.

3 Combine and mix sesame mixture with spaghetti. Sprinkle white sesame seeds on top and serve hot.

SPAGHETTI WITH BLACK SESAME SAUCE
黒ごまのスパゲッティ

CHAPTER EIGHT
DESERTS 創

DORAYAKI
どらやき

HOME AWAY FROM HOME
SERVES 4

4	eggs
1 cup	sugar
2 tbsp.	honey
2¼ cups	flour
1 cup	water
1 tsp.	baking soda
2 cups	anko

1 Mix together eggs, sugar and honey.

2 Add flour, water and baking soda.

3 Over medium heat with a non-stick pan, put a tablespoon of batter and spread into a round shape. Cook until it browns, then turn over and cook 30 seconds. Repeat with remaining batter. Ensure you finish with an even number of pancakes.

4 Take a spoonful of anko and place between two pancakes with browned sides facing out.

5 Allow to cool for a few minutes. Afterwards, wrap with plastic wrap.

Out of the many recipes for dorayaki, this recipe given to Tonari Gumi from the late Mrs. Tokiko Watanabe, was by far, the best. Everyone at Tonari Gumi remembers Tokiko with affection and gratitude.

2½ cups	milk
1½ cups	sugar
¾ cup	vegetable oil
3	eggs
1 tsp.	baking powder
2½ cups	mochiko
2 cups	anko

1 Preheat oven to 180°C.

2 Mix milk, sugar, vegetable oil, eggs, baking powder and mochiko in a blender.

3 Set aside ⅔ of the mochi mixture.

4 To the remaining ⅓, add anko and mix well.

5 Spread the remaining ⅔ of the mochi mixture in a 9 by 13 inch cake pan.

6 Snaking back and forth, drop anko mixture on top of mochi mixture.

7 Bake in the oven for about 1 hour. Cut into squares and serve at room temperature.

MATCHA CHIFFON CAKE
抹茶シフォンケーキ

SERVES 10

1½ cups	flour
1½ cups	sugar
1 tbsp.	baking powder
1 tsp.	salt
2 tbsp.	matcha
½ cup	vegetable oil
7	egg yolks
¾ cup	water
1 tsp.	vanilla extract
1 cup	egg whites
½ tsp.	Crème of Tartar

1 Preheat oven to 165°C.

2 Mix together flour, sugar, baking powder, salt and matcha in a bowl.

3 In a separate bowl, mix vegetable oil, egg yolks, water and vanilla extract.

4 Combine dry ingredients and wet ingredients and mix well.

5 Whip egg whites with Crème of Tartar until stiff peaks form and gently fold into mixture.

6 Pour in chiffon cake pan and bake for 50 minutes.

7 Raise oven temperatue to 180°C and bake another 15 minutes.

8 Remove from oven and invert pan. Let it cool.

½ pkg.	tofu (about 200 g.)
1¼ cups	mochiko
4 tbsp.	yomogi powder (about 20 g.)
½ cup	hot water
2 cups	anko

1 Mix tofu and mochiko together. Because of variations in the amount of water in tofu, first add ¾ cup of mochiko, and then add the remainder little by little until dough reaches desired consistency. The dough should be about as hard as an earlobe, and mochiko shouldn't come off on hands.

2 Dissolve yomogi powder in hot water. Gently squeeze water out and into dough.

3 In a pot, boil some water. Take one tablespoon of dough and form into a ball. Repeat for remaining dough. Drop balls of dough into boiling water. After dough rises to the surface, wait 1 minute, then remove and place on a tea towel to remove excess water.

4 Poke a toothpick into two dango. Place a small amount of anko on top and serve.

TOFU DANGO
豆腐団子

KASUTERA
カステラ

SERVES 8

Kasutera is a Japanese pound cake

9	egg whites
¾ cup	sugar
9	egg yolks
3 tbsp.	corn syrup
¾ cup	sugar
2 tbsp.	vegetable oil
1½ cups	flour

1 Preheat oven to 180°C.

2 Beat egg whites and gradually add sugar. Beat until stiff peaks form and set aside.

3 Mix egg yolks, syrup, sugar and vegetable oil together. Add flour and mix well.

4 Combine egg white and egg yolk mixtures to form batter.

5 Pour batter into a 9 by 13 inch cake pan with bottom lined with wax paper.

6 Bake for 40 minutes on the middle rack.

7 Turn off heat and let cake sit in oven for 5 minutes.

8 Remove and immediately place cake upside down onto wax paper.

9 Though cake can be cut and served, keeping in a sealed container for a couple of days before serving will improve taste.

Recipe variation: To make Matcha Kasutera, add 4 tsp. of matcha tea powder during step 3 when adding flour.

1 box	gelatin (4 pouches totalling 28 g.)
¾ cup	sugar
1 can	mango pulp (750 ml)
500 ml	whipping cream

1 Dissolve gelatin in ½ cup of water. Add 1 cup of hot water. Mix well.

2 Add sugar to 2½ cups of hot water.

3 Mix mango pulp and whipping cream. Add gelatin mixture and sugar water. Mix until well combined.

4 Pour into a 9 by 13 inch pan or into individual glasses and leave in refrigerator for about 3 hours before serving.

MANGO PUDDING

マンゴープリン

SESAME COOKIES

ごまのクッキー

HOME AWAY FROM HOME

SERVES 5

¾ cup	vegetable oil
¾ cup	sugar
1	egg
1¾ cup	flour, sifted
1 tsp.	baking powder
pinch	salt
¾ cup	black and white sesame seeds

1 Preheat oven to 180°C.

2 Whip vegetable oil with mixer and add sugar little by little.

3 Add egg and continue mixing.

4 Combine flour, baking powder and salt. Add flour mixture a third at a time and mix well.

5 Add sesame seeds and continue mixing.

6 Flatten dough and freeze.

7 Defrost dough and taking a tablespoonful at a time, form dough into balls. Place on cookie sheet and flatten.

8 Bake for about 15 minutes.

SERVES 10

6	eggs
1 cup	flour
¾ cup	cornstarch
½ lb.	unsalted butter
1¼ cups	sugar
to taste	rum

Icing:

1	egg white
2 cups	icing sugar
½ tsp.	lemon juice
½ tsp.	rum

1 Preheat oven to broil and have a rack set in the middle.

2 Take 4 of the 6 eggs and separate into whites and yolks.

3 Beat 4 egg whites in a bowl and set aside.

4 Mix flour and cornstarch in a bowl.

5 Beat butter until it turns white. Add sugar, 2 whole eggs, 4 egg yolks, flour and cornstarch mixture and rum to taste. Mix well. Add 4 egg whites and mix again.

6 In a 22 cm round cake pan with removable bottom, bake cake one thin layer at a time for about 3-4 minutes for each layer or until done. Repeat until batter is used up. Remove from pan. Let it cool.

7 For icing, beat egg white and add icing sugar, lemon juice and rum.

BAUM KUCHEN
バームクーヘン

AFGHAN COOKIES
アフガンクッキー

HOME AWAY FROM HOME

SERVES 5

1 cup	butter (or half butter & half margarine)
¼ cup	sugar
1 tsp.	vanilla extract
1½ cups	flour
1 tsp.	baking powder
¼ cup	unsweetened cocoa powder
2 cups	cornflakes, slightly crushed nuts, for topping

Icing:

1 cup	icing sugar
2 tsp.	unsweetened cocoa powder

1 Preheat oven to 180°C.

2 Cream butter and sugar until soft and light and add vanilla extract.

3 Sift together flour, baking powder and cocoa powder. Add to butter mixture and stir.

4 Add and mix cornflakes.

5 Place parchment on a cookie sheet. Take a tablespoon of batter, form a ball and put on cookie sheet. Flatten ball with a fork.

6 Bake in oven for about 20 minutes until firm to the touch.

7 Combine ingredients for icing and mix well. Add water if needed. When cookies have cooled, dab icing on top and sprinkle on nuts.

Note: Very little sugar is used in the cookie dough and the cornflakes add a crunchy texture. No eggs are used in this recipe.

½ cup	butter
½ cup	margarine
½ cup	sugar
½ cup	brown sugar
1	egg, beaten
1 tsp.	vanilla
1¼ cups	flour
½ tsp.	baking powder
½ tsp.	baking soda
1 cup	oatmeal
½ cup	coconut
1 cup	Rice Krispies®
½ cup	mini chocolate chips

1 Preheat oven to 180°C.

2 Mix together butter, margarine, sugar, brown sugar, egg and vanilla.

3 Sift together flour, baking powder and baking soda.

4 Add flour mixture to butter mixture. Mix well.

5 Mix in oatmeal, coconut, Rice Krispies® and chocolate chips.

6 Take a tablespoon of mixture, form a ball and place on a cookie sheet lined with parchment paper. Flatten ball with a fork.

7 Bake for 10-15 minutes.

HARVEST COOKIES

ハーベストクッキー

BROKEN GLASS DESSERT

ブロークングラスデザート

SERVES 8

Graham wafer crust:

1⅓ cups	graham wafer crumbs
⅓ cup	sugar
⅓ cup	butter, melted
1 tsp.	cinnamon

Filling:

1 pkg.	red Jell-O®
1 pkg.	lime Jell-O®
1 pkg.	lemon Jell-O®
2 cups	whipping cream
½ cup	sugar
1 bag	unflavored gelatin (7 g.)
1 can	crushed pineapple

1 Mix ingredients for graham wafer crust and press into 9 by 13 inch pan. Chill.

2 For filling, dissolve each package of Jell-O® powder in 1½ cups hot water in separate pans. Chill and when solid, cut into small squares.

3 Lightly whip cream. Add sugar and beat until stiff.

4 Soften gelatin in ½ cup water. Add ½ cup hot water and stir to dissolve gelatin. Let it cool.

5 Mix whipped cream, gelatin and crushed pineapple. Next, gently add Jell-O® into mixture.

6 Pour onto the chilled crust. Leave overnight in refrigerator. Cut into squares and serve.

1 can	Mandarin oranges, drained & chopped (325 ml)
1 can	crushed pineapples, drained (590 ml)
2 cups	seedless green grapes
1 cup	shredded coconut (medium sweetened)
2 cups	miniature marshmallows
2 cups	sour cream

Mix all ingredients and refrigerate overnight. The fruits should be well-drained. Serve in glasses.

Making Anko

2 cups azuki (300 g.), 300 g. sugar

Wash azuki and soak in water overnight. Drain, then boil in ample water. During boiling, add water if needed. Occasionally skim top. Cook until beans are soft enough to break open with fingers. In the meantime, place a dish cloth over a bowl. When azuki is soft enough, filter with the dish cloth. Wrap beans with the dish cloth and squeeze out as much excess water as possible. Place azuki in a pot over medium-high heat and add sugar. Keep stirring with a wooden spatula to prevent sugar from burning. Continue to do so until paste thickens. Remove from heat and place on a dish cloth lined on a baking tray to cool.

AMBROSIA
アンブロージア

DAIFUKU MOCHI

大福餅

SERVES 8

4 cups	anko
2 cups	mochiko
2 cups + **2 tbsp.**	water
2 cups	sugar
½ tsp.	salt
as needed	cornstarch

1 Take a small amount of anko and form into a ball. Make 30 balls in total.

2 Mix mochiko and water well in a heat-resistant glass bowl. Cover with plastic wrap and microwave for 4 minutes.

3 Remove from microwave and mix with a wooden spoon. Cover with plastic wrap again, poke a few holes and microwave once more for 4 minutes.

4 Remove from microwave and add sugar and salt to mixture. Mix thoroughly. Toss mixture with two wooden spoons about 200 times. Or, another way is to pound with a wooden stick, dipping the wooden stick in water when it gets sticky. Toss or pound mixture until it becomes white and smooth.

5 Lightly flour a cutting board with cornstarch. Place dough onto board and roll into a cylinder. Divide into 30 pieces and wrap each piece completely around a ball of anko by stretching dough.

Note: This is a very easy way to prepare mochi-manju. You can also put a strawberry in the anko and wrap it inside to create a strawberry daifuku.

APPENDIX 創

ABURA-AGE: Sliced, deep-fried tofu.

AMI: Salted shrimp flavouring sold in bottles.

ANKO: A dark red, sweet bean paste made from red azuki beans.

AONORI: A type of edible green seaweed.

ATSUYAKI TAMAGO: Japanese omelet with seasonings that is rolled into a thick layer in a rectangular pan.

AZUKI: A small, reddish bean with a sweet flavor. Used for soups, desserts and anko.

BAMBOO SUSHI MAT: A rollable bamboo sheet that is used to make maki-sushi or roll-sushi.

BLACK BEAN SAUCE: A dark sauce made from soybeans which is then salted and fermented.

CHIKUWA: Fish paste formed into a tube-like shape with a bamboo stick and grilled. Used in various dishes such as oden or nimono.

CURRY ROUX: Pre-packaged curry which can be used out-of-the-box by adding hot water. It comes in hot, medium and mild roux varieties.

DAIKON: Japanese white radish.

DANGO: Japanese dumpling made from rice flour.

DASHI: Japanese soup stock, the base of many Japanese dishes. See page 111 for recipes on how to make dashi.

DASHI-NO-MOTO: Japanese soup base sold in instant form as a powder.

EDAMAME: Green soy beans. Available frozen.

GOBO: Burdock root. Available in most Asian groceries and specialty shops.

HAKUSAI: Also known as Chinese cabbage, nappa cabbage or celery cabbage.

JAPANESE CUCUMBER: Known in Japan as kyuri, it is available in Asian markets and specialty shops.

JAPANESE EGGPLANT: Also known as nasu or aubergine.

JAPANESE RICE: Short-grain rice with a higher starch content than long or medium-grain varieties. Becomes sticky when cooked. See page 137 for more details.

KABOCHA: Hard and shaped like a squat pumpkin. The outside is a dark green and the inside is orange. When cooked, the flesh is sweet and tender.

KEZURIBUSHI: Boiled then dried bonito that has been shaved into fine strands or short flakes.

KONBU: Used heavily in Japanese cuisine, it is one of the basic ingredients of dashi (soup stock). It is a long, dark-brown seaweed that is covered in a white powder-like coating that delivers considerable flavour to soup stock.

KONYAKU: A translucent, gelatinous cake produced from a yamlike vegetable known as Devil's Tongue. Has no discernable flavour and comes in white and black types.

MANJU: Not made of rice flour but rather other varieties such as wheat flour, buckwheat flour, etc. Usually has filling such as anko inside and is baked or steamed.

MATCHA POWDER: Bright, powdered green tea that is used in the Japanese tea ceremony. Also known as hikicha.

MIRIN: Japanese sweet rice wine used for cooking. Has a distinctive yellow colour.

MISO: Fermented bean paste. Comes in different colours and flavours. There are three varieties: barley miso, rice miso and soybean miso. A healthy addition to any diet, it can be found in Japanese sauces, soups, main dishes, salad dressings and as a condiment.

MOCHIKO: Sweet rice flour.

NATTO: Fermented soybeans. Sold in single-serving sizes. Often eaten over rice.

NORI: Dried seaweed. Sold in sheets.

OKARA: A white pulp that is left behind after the liquid is drained while making soy milk. High in fibre and protein, it is used in a number of Japanese dishes from soups to salads.

RENKON: Lotus root.

SAKE: Japanese rice wine used in cooking. Can be purchased at most liquor stores and at Asian grocery stores.

SAKURA DENBU: Dried codfish flakes with pink colouring.

SHIITAKE MUSHROOMS: Also known as Chinese black mushrooms or black forest mushrooms.

SOBA: Thin Japanese buckwheat noodles.

SURIMI: Fish paste that is formed into various shapes. It usually consists of Alaskan Pollock or Pacific Whiting.

SUSHI RICE: Rice that is made with a mixture of vinegar, sugar and salt for use with sushi. It is also referred to sushi meshi.

TENKASU: The left-over crunchy bits from the deep-fried batter used for tempura. Often used to garnish udon soup and okonomiyaki.

TOBANJAN: Spicy miso bean sauce. Sold in bottles.

WAKAME: Available both dried and fresh, it is a dark green edible seaweed. Used in simmered dishes and soups, it is very popular in Japan and Asian countries where it is often used like a vegetable.

WASABI: Japanese horseradish. Found most commonly in the form of a condiment for consumption with sushi. Known for its strong, spicy flavour, it has found its way into salad dressings and sauces. Use like mustard.

YAKISOBA NOODLES: Wheat-based noodles sold fresh or in vacuum packs.

YOMOGI POWDER: Mugwort powder. Used in Japanese sweets such as manju and dango.

All equivalents have been rounded for convenience.

LENGTH

Imperial	Metric
⅛ inch	3 millimeters
¼ inch	6 millimeters
½ inch	12 millimeters
1 inch	2.5 centimeters

LIQUID / DRY MEASURES

Imperial	Metric
¼ teaspoon	1.25 millilitres
½ teaspoon	2.5 millilitres
1 teaspoon	5 millilitres
1 tablespoon (3 teaspoons)	15 millilitres
1 fluid ounce (2 tablespoons)	30 millilitres
¼ cup	60 millilitres
⅓ cup	80 millilitres
½ cup	120 millilitres
1 cup	240 millilitres
1 pint (2 cups)	480 millilitres
1 quart (4 cups, 32 ounces)	960 millilitres
1 gallon (4 quarts)	3.84 liters
1 ounce (by weight)	28 grams
1 pound (by weight)	454 grams
2.2 pounds	1 kilogram

OVEN TEMPERATURE

Fahrenheit	Celsius	Gas
250	120	½
275	140	1
300	150	2
325	160	3
350	180	4
375	190	5
400	200	6
425	220	7
450	230	8
475	240	9
500	260	10

INDEX OF RECIPES